THE ABC'S OF MAKING BUSINESS NETWORKING WORK FOR YOU

Dr. Sinclair N. Grey III

Copyright © 2016 Dr. Sinclair N. Grey III

All rights reserved.

ISBN-13: 978-1535376433

No part of this book may be reproduced, stored in a retrieval system or transmitted in any form or by any means without the prior written permission of the publisher, except by a reviewer who may quote brief passages in a review to be printed in a newspaper, magazine, or journal.

Dr. Sinclair N. Grey III
www.sinclairgrey.org
678.516.0779

DEDICATION

This book is dedicated to every entrepreneur who made the decision to go into business for himself/herself. Because entrepreneurship requires hard work, commitment, and dedication, it's important that each entrepreneur is equipped with the necessary tools to remain active.

With that said, I dedicate this book to every entrepreneur and to those who are striving to be their own boss.

ACKNOWLEDGMENTS

First and foremost, I have to thank God for allowing me to write a book that will help every entrepreneur to become more successful in their business.

Secondly, I want to thank the love of my life, Kimberly Hudson for her continuous support and encouragement. Without her help, this book would have not been written in clear terms.

Last but not least, I want to thank all of my business connections I've made throughout the world. Your wealth of knowledge continues to make me better each day, professionally and personally.

THE ABC'S OF MAKING BUSINESS NETWORKING WORK FOR YOU
INTRODUCTION

In today's business world, it's vitally important you understand the importance of networking. This is not to an attempt to down, degrade, or diminish the need for knowledge, skill, and ability in which your business operates, but the truth of the matter is whenever a person overlooks, neglects, and undervalues, networking, one will find himself/herself struggling to find work, contracts, and the right connection that will open doors of opportunity.

In this book, I will teach you the ABC's on how to make business networking work for you. This isn't by no means the end all be all, but it is a way to help you become more productive in business. Let's face it – the more productive you are in business, the more prosperous you'll see your business and the bottom line.

As an entrepreneur, I have throughout my business career seen the value of networking. Just about every client I obtained was through someone I met and established a good relationship with. It's through cultivating a healthy relationship that you stand out in the crowd. In a real sense, when you take the right approach to networking, you discover that people are drawn to you because of other people.

THE ABC'S OF MAKING BUSINESS NETWORKING WORK FOR YOU
ATTITUDE

According to Dictionary.com, the word 'attitude' is defined as "A manner, disposition, feeling, position, etc., with regard to a person or thing; tendency or orientation, especially of the mind." Let me make it plain and relevant to business networking. Unless you approach networking with the right attitude or should I say, a positive attitude, you won't be able to see its benefits and advantages.

Successful entrepreneurs don't see networking as a job. They view is as fun, exciting, and a way of meeting new people. It all starts with your attitude. If you approach networking as something that's bothersome and overwhelming, your demeanor will become manifested upon your arrival and talk.

Why not see networking as a means to which you can do three things: 1. Help someone who needs your help, 2. Establish new friendships/relationships, and 3. Allow someone who has what you need to help you in return.

Going back to the definition of 'attitude,' it says it's a feeling. That's right; it's a feeling you control. If those around you don't have a positive feeling of networking, you need to find others who display a positive attitude. Always remember, the energy people give off around you is contagious. That's why you don't want anyone around you that's lackluster, complaining, and depressed within your circle.

The other part of the definition is position. Unless you position yourself around the right people in the right place, your attitude will be diminished. Whatever your profession, you can always find people who need your product and/or service. Don't let discouragement hinder you. In addition to this, don't let the opinions of people who don't do what you do get you off track.

THE ABC'S OF MAKING BUSINESS NETWORKING WORK FOR YOU
BUSINESS CARD ETIQUETTE

What does your business card say about you? Does it distinguish you from your competitors or does it put you in the same category? Your business card is a tool by which people remember you by and will thereby help increase your chances of getting a follow up phone call and/or email.

Whenever you decide to order your business cards, make sure the following happens.

- The paper is of good quality. Nothing cheap.

- Make sure your name/title/phone number, address, and email address is easily readable. Using fonts that cause a person to strain their eyes is never a good idea.

- If possible, use the back of the business card to list what you do offer (services and/or products).

- Include your picture. People may not remember names, but they remember faces.

I need to make a note here: leave the postcards at your office. No one wants to walk around holding a postcard while they are trying to network.

THE ABC'S OF MAKING BUSINESS NETWORKING WORK FOR YOU
CONFIDENCE

An entrepreneur who fails to exude confidence when networking is a person who creates doubt. One thing you need to do is believe in your business and in what you offer. If you're not sure that you can solve a problem, then the people you meet will be hesitant in doing business with you.

Being confident is more than articulating what you do, it's your non-verbal skills that come into play. Do you look timid and/or uncertain? Are you willing to look a person in the eye while communicating? And does your body language tell people you're a winner? Let's face it – confidence separates winners from losers. I want you to understand this important point – one who is confident doesn't have to be arrogant. There is a difference. One who is confident knows who they are and needs no validation from those on the outside. On the other hand, one who is arrogant seeks to show off thereby creating an illusion of uncertainty. To be quite frank, arrogance is a turn off when networking.

I've been to my fair share of networking events and I can tell you that I'm drawn to confident people. They are the ones I want to know and help. You must remember this – networking is about building relationships that last. It's not about getting a quick sale.

Here are some ways to boost your confidence when networking:

- Talk to yourself before you begin networking and say these words, 'I'm important, I matter, I'm good at what I do, and I'm a confident person.'

- Understand people embrace a confident person. Distinguish yourself by your verbal and non-verbal skills.

- Smile when talking to people. Through smiling, you're not only sending the message to others that you're happy to meet them, but you're also letting them know they are interacting with a confident person.

- Dress to impress. Looking good translates to feeling good.

Don't feel the need to compete with other entrepreneurs. Confident networkers are not concerned about the quantity of business cards collected, they are concerned with the quality of connections made.

THE ABC'S OF MAKING BUSINESS NETWORKING WORK FOR YOU
DETERMINATION

If you're not determined to make business networking a part of your weekly routine, you're missing so much. Let me back up for a moment and clarify something. Weekly business networking keeps you sharp and in front of potential clients/customers. You should never view weekly business networking as a drag because it isn't.

As an entrepreneur, you can't afford to take any time off. You must continue to establish new connections. With that said, you can't spend all of your time at events that you fail to follow up. As one of my mentors in business told me years ago, 'if you're serious about being successful, you have to have determination.' If I were to simplify it a little more, I would say those who are determined to 'blow up from the floor up' refuse to make excuses for why something can't be done.

Every week, I make it a point to attend at least three business networking events. Through these events, I meet new people and reconnect with those I met previously. By the way, every event you attend doesn't have to be costly. You can use www.meetup.com to find networking events in your area.

Now you may be asking yourself, how do I get this determination? Here's how:

- Ask yourself the question – what is the end result (new business, new connections, or a new friend)

- Consider how your business will grow, if you don't have determination. I want you to get this in your spirit – your business should be growing in every direction.

- Have an accountability partner. This person needs to be someone you trust and has your best interest in mind. They will be the one who refuses to hear excuses.

- Refuse to quit. Every successful entrepreneur has faced disappointments. Just because you face disappointments, it doesn't mean you're a failure. Here's a hint – use disappointments and fear as motivation for your elevation.

THE ABC'S OF MAKING BUSINESS NETWORKING WORK FOR YOU
EDUCATION

You don't have to spend a lot of money getting an MBA degree to become educated in networking. Don't get me wrong, education is important and without a doubt, it should be obtained and acquired because it's the 'new commodity.' However, I want to be clear in stating that education in this sense is having a firm understanding of world events.

Those who know the power of networking are able to speak on various issues that have nothing to do with their business. It's impressive if you're well-read in world affairs. It makes the conversation flow smoothly.

Those who are educated will understand the do's and don'ts about business interactions, how to speak to people, how to conduct meetings, and how to think logically and clearly. In addition to that, those who value education will think outside of the box.

Here's how you can improve and enhance your education when it comes to networking:

- Read the local newspaper as well as financial papers. Through reading, studying, and analyzing, you become knowledgeable and more informed of trends happening in the world.

- Research your business networking group. Find out who attends the group, the vision of the group, how long the group has been established, and what you can bring to the group.

- Don't be afraid to voice your concerns on topics. Warning: make sure you can back up your point(s) with facts and data. Personal opinion is okay, but a well-informed networker attracts people to them.

- Learn from other people on how they network. Books are good tools, but unless you implement and apply what you've read, it's not going to work. Please note: every business networking event takes skill.

Education is a daily process. Never stop learning because when you stop learning, you stop growing. Your business is too valuable for you not to learn.

THE ABC'S OF MAKING BUSINESS NETWORKING WORK FOR YOU

FOLLOW UP

Now that you have collected someone's business card, what are you going to do with it? Are you going to take a picture of it on your smartphone with an app that stores business cards? Will you put the card in a file that you'll look at every now and then? Will you even follow up with a call and/or email?

The importance of following up with someone who gave you their business card is **YOUR RESPONSIBILITY**. Let me repeat that. **YOU HAVE TO BE THE ONE** who reaches out to the person. If you're sitting back waiting for someone to contact you, you may or may not hear from them. Too many people make it a habit of collecting business cards without ever doing anything with them. If you really want to succeed in your business, you have to follow up. As one of my mentors told me years ago, 'the fortune is in the follow up.'

You may be thinking that follow up can become too cumbersome or a waste of time, however, I want you to think about this – what's going to happen if you don't follow up? Your competitors will. And here's something else to think about. If you don't plan on following up with people you meet at networking events, don't go. That's right; don't waste your time and the time of others if you're not going to be proactive.

Those who are serious about following up need to do the following:

- Write on the back of every card you collect where you met the person and something of interest the both of you spoke about. It will rekindle your memory when you meet.

- Send an email within 24 hours stating that it was a pleasure meeting the individual. Don't make it sound too general, personalize it.

- Do not try to sell the individual via email. It's a turn off.

- Request a meeting so that you can learn about the individual, their business, and how you can help them. Once again, the follow up meeting isn't about selling; it's about learning about the individual. I want you to understand this important point – people do business with people they know, like, and trust.

- Don't get frustrated if you don't get an immediate response. Persistence pays off; just don't be pushy.

Think of helping the other person. The more you help someone achieve their goals, the more you'll receive in return. It's called Karma.

THE ABC'S OF MAKING BUSINESS NETWORKING WORK FOR YOU

GOALS

Every time you attend a networking event, you should have a goal. Without setting goals for yourself, you're simply going around in a circle going nowhere. Goals help you stay focused on achieving what you want to achieve. Think about it for a moment. You have goals for your business (e.g. how many clients you want each month, how much revenue you want to make, and how long it will take to expand your business). Each goal requires more commitment. It's through your commitment that you become successful at networking.

Let me ask you a question. When you attend networking events, do you establish goals such as how many people you want to connect with or how many follow up meetings you want to have? Every time you attend a meeting, there should be some goals.

Here's an example. I attended a networking meeting one afternoon before I was scheduled to be on a radio show and the host of the event asked each participant what is your goal? Because I knew just about everyone in the room and their business, I told the group my goal was to meet someone new that I hadn't met and to set up an appointment with them over coffee/tea. Very clear and concise. Well, I did just that and I was able to set up two appointments. My goal wasn't to sell them anything; it was an opportunity to find out who they were and what they did. By the way, because of that, I was able to gain their business at a later time.

Here are a few suggestions on setting goals for each networking event you attend:

- Ask yourself how many people you would like to connect with? Be as specific as possible.

- How many following meetings can you establish? In other words, how many appointments/follow up meetings can you make on the spot?

- Set out to arrive early to meet early arrivers.

- Make a list of business categories you're seeking to do business with.

THE ABC'S OF MAKING BUSINESS NETWORKING WORK FOR YOU
HELP

If you really want to make a good impression on someone, offer to help them. I want you to understand that I'm not talking about being a constructive criticizer; I'm speaking of helping a person meet someone who might be interested in their product and/or service. Let's face it – many of us are where we are today in business because someone saw potential in us and offered help. Because of their unselfish act, we should be doing the same thing as often as possible.

Helping someone at a networking event may seem a bit strange in the beginning because so many people have the mindset of it's all about me, it's about getting new business, and it's about showing off. That's not going to get you far in business. When you take time to help those who are networking like yourself, you stand out from the crowd because you're a person who cares about the success of other people.

While living in Maryland, I would attend one particular event every Thursday. During this event, there were probably 50 to 60 people in attendance and it was our assignment to listen to an individuals' needs and introduce them to someone in the room who could fulfill that need. To most of you reading this, this is odd but after you stop to think about it for a moment, it teaches you the art of listening and connecting. As soon as I would meet someone who could fulfill a particular need of someone else I had just met, I would do a warm introduction of the two individuals and leave. That's right; with a warm introduction I've just helped two people.

Here's how you can separate yourself at a networking event by simply helping.

- Listen carefully to what someone is telling you about their business.

- Ask questions for further clarification.

- Write down on their business card what needs to be done.

As you meet people who can fulfill the need, make the introduction yourself. Let me be very clear about this. Walk the person over to the one you just met and introduce them. Remember, with your introduction be confident.

THE ABC'S OF MAKING BUSINESS NETWORKING WORK FOR YOU
INITIATE

If you're going to wait in a corner for someone to come over to start a conversation with you, you better think again. That's right; you need to think twice about waiting for someone to make the move.

As an entrepreneur, you need to be the one who initiates a conversation. It's not being pushy, it's being confident. When you stop to think about it for a moment, many people attend networking events without knowing a whole lot of people in attendance. They may know a few people and that's it. As one business owner told me, 'I hate going to networking events whereby I don't know a single person in the room.' My response was that's a perfect time to meet someone new so you won't have that feeling anymore.

Initiating conversation with other entrepreneurs sends a direct as well as indirect message you're willing to go after what you want. You can't be in business for long, if you have a passive mentality. I want you to ponder on this – you go to networking events to meet people, not to hold up space.

Here are some ways you can initiate conversations with other business networkers:

- Quickly scan the room to find people standing by themselves and looking lost, confused, and/or overwhelmed. Be the person who approaches them with light conversation by making them feel at ease.

- Begin the conversation with something other than business. Try asking your fellow entrepreneur how their day is going, how was their weekend, or how are they doing, in general. Most networkers are so accustomed to the standard business questions that it's often good to change the routine.

- Carefully observe the room of attendees and see who needs help with something. For example, if someone is having a hard time doing something, go over and offer to be of assistance.

There's nothing wrong with showing initiative. Because of what has been highlighted, it may seem as though you're the aggressor and that's okay. If you're not sure of what you want, then you'll find it difficult obtaining what you want.

THE ABC'S OF MAKING BUSINESS NETWORKING WORK FOR YOU
JOURNALING

Just about everyone has a smartphone and because of that, there's an app on the phone called Notes. I mentioned earlier that you need to write something about the person on their business card, but journaling in your Note application allows you to write more, to remember more, and to have it at your fingertips.

In addition to journaling information about a new contact, you need to also journal your thoughts about the event. What went well and what didn't go well. Don't be lazy or procrastinate about journaling.

Here are a couple of suggestions about journaling.

- Keep your notes clear and concise. You don't want to have trouble reading what you wrote.

- Let the other person know you're going to take notes. Whenever someone sees you're interested in them, they are more inclined to do business with you.

I want you to understand this – if you're too busy trying to memorize everything, you're bound to forget something. Take an extra minute or two to make some notes (journal). It could be the difference between walking into a large account or losing a deal.

THE ABC'S OF MAKING BUSINESS NETWORKING WORK FOR YOU
KNOWLEDGE

Unless you know what you're offering, you will look foolish. Wait a minute, let me back up a moment. If you don't know your industry, what does that say about your willingness to solve a problem. In addition to this, without knowing and understanding your industry, your credibility will be called into question.

Do your own research. While it's good to relay information you heard from your colleagues, you have to do your own due diligence. Business owners and in this case, decision makers appreciate people who are current with all that's happening in the business world. Remember, your job isn't to sell a person during networking, it's your time to meet, greet, and converse.

Here's an interesting story. I went to a networking event about a year ago and a gentleman approached me trying to sell me his service. During his sales pitch, I stopped him and told him that I wasn't signing up for anything until I had a chance to do my own research. Needless to say, this didn't stop him and he continued being persistent with his pitch. I continued to let him talk and within a few moments, I discovered he didn't know what he was talking about because he didn't do his proper research. After I told him his error, he didn't apologize but said, I was told this would work by someone.

Again, I have to stress the point, if you don't know what you're talking about, don't go to a networking event. If you're not confident in what you're talking about, stay home, practice, and then show up ready to network. People can see through the fake and phony.

Here are some ways to acquire knowledge:

- Read, read, and read as much as you can about your product and/or service.

- Talk to people who are successful in your industry. As my mentor would say, 'pick their brain.'

- Share your information with your colleagues and ask for their opinion. They will tell you how well you know your product and/or service. Ask them to observe your body language to see what you're really conveying (non-verbally)

THE ABC'S OF MAKING BUSINESS NETWORKING WORK FOR YOU
LEARN

There's a biblical proverb that says, "Intelligent people want to learn but stupid people are satisfied with ignorance." Unless someone is willing to learn what to do and what not to do, they will find themselves going in a circle ending up nowhere.

Entrepreneurs must constantly learn how to network. Even though someone may be skilled in many areas, - learning must continually take place. Every interaction is a learning experience. Never assume you know everything because you don't.

Successful entrepreneurs use every moment to learn. That's right; within every networking environment, you can learn about the setup of the room. You learn how people interact with one another. And you learn what people value most about their business.

Here are some ways to learn better:

- Observe your surroundings. Unless you observe your surroundings, you won't know how to act and/or react.

- Don't be afraid to ask questions. A person who is unwilling to ask questions is a person who refuses to learn.

- Ditch the 'I KNOW IT ALL ATTITUDE.' Those who think they know it all, don't know anything. In fact, they are really ignorant because they are too prideful.

Before every networking encounter, ask yourself the question, 'what do I want to learn today?'

THE ABC'S OF MAKING BUSINESS NETWORKING WORK FOR YOU
MAGNETIC APPEAL

If one looks at what a magnet is and does, one will conclude that a magnet draws/attracts that which it comes into contact with. A magnet can only draw something that has the same magnetic force. In other words, a magnet cannot draw that which is opposite from its makeup.

Entrepreneurs need to be a magnetic force so that others can be drawn to them. Once an entrepreneur learns how to be a magnet that attracts, they will begin to see their business prosper, their popularity soar, and their network increase. I need to pen this warning – if you don't want your business to grow and if you're not willing to accept the responsibility that comes with it, GET OUT. Entrepreneurs who are constantly drawing the right people to them understand they are accountable for their work. Permit me to use another term. Magnetic entrepreneurs realize they have a gift and are not afraid to use it.

Future customers/clients are drawn to people who represent their business in a professional manner.

Here are some ways to have magnetic appeal:

- Dress appropriately. How a person dresses for networking functions can draw or deter. From head to toe, people are watching and observing you.

- Speak with confidence. To say it more plainly – use good English and know what you're talking about.

- Smile. People are drawn to smiles and it will bring down any defensive walls.

- Listen and make eye-contact.

THE ABC'S OF MAKING BUSINESS NETWORKING WORK FOR YOU
NAME TAG

We've already discussed why having a professional looking business card is important in networking. Now I want to share with you why wearing a name tag is important.

Before I begin, when I say wear a name tag, I'm not speaking of the peel off name tag that so many people wear at networking events. Those peel off name tags are not professional. Think about it. You simply write your name and possibly your company name on it. [Hope you have good penmanship]. In addition to that, you hope it stays on your shirt or jacket.

A professional name tag should have your name and company engraved on it. Professionalism at its best.

Here's what a professional name tag does:

- It causes you to stand out in the crowd. [Remember, you need magnetic appeal].

- Easy to read and you don't have to worry about it falling or peeling off.

- When placed on your lapel, people will be able to see it and therefore initiate a dialogue.

Networking can be fun and it's up to you to make it so. Being creative shows others you think outside the box. Let me tell you this – when I started this practice, it made conversations a lot easier which has led to good friendships as well as good contracts.

THE ABC'S OF MAKING BUSINESS NETWORKING WORK FOR YOU
OPENNESS

If you're shy about meeting potential clients/customers, you're leaving money on the table. On the other hand, this isn't the time to ask people for the sale.

People like to ask questions and if you're unable to answer someone's question effectively and efficiently, you're not open. Being closed-minded will keep you frustrated, aggravated, and broke.

Those who are open at networking events are fun to talk to and with. They share funny stories and give individuals a peek into who they are as a person. Entrepreneurs like to do business with people who are real, relevant, and transparent (to some degree). I'm not saying to tell your life story to someone who you just met, however, you do need to be open and speak on topics other than business.

Here are some ways in which you can be open:

- Have fun. In other words, keep the conversation light and crack some jokes.

- Realize you are interesting. You don't have to be stuffy.

- Share past experiences that have helped you become better with others.

THE ABC'S OF MAKING BUSINESS NETWORKING WORK FOR YOU

PASSION

Let's face it – if you're not passionate about your business, don't expect others to take you seriously. When one is passionate about what they do, it's contagious. Isn't that what you want as an entrepreneur? For people to see your passion, hear your passion, and feel your passion.

Think about the many networking events you've attended to only hear people with no passion. How did it make you feel? Did you want to do business with them? Did you even want to talk to them? People who are passionate about what they do draw the right people to them.

Entrepreneurs go into business because they love what they do and want to make a prosperous living from doing so. In the beginning, the passion is strong. However, as time passes, the passion one had in the beginning can lessen. The challenge is to keep the passion at all times. Remember, when your passion declines so does your ability to attract the right kind of clients.

Before attending networking events make sure you're passionate about meeting people, sharing your business, and learning from people. Because networking can be draining at times, it's best to meditate and gather your thoughts before entering a venue. I promise you this – if you gather your thoughts and understand your passion, you'll find success.

Here are some ways you can have passion:

- Relax your mind before attending any event.
- Remind yourself why you went into business for yourself.
- Talk to yourself and affirm your self-worth.

THE ABC'S OF MAKING BUSINESS NETWORKING WORK FOR YOU
QUALITY

Let me explain this to you. You can attend many networking events, gather a lot of business cards, meet a lot people and not receive any quality leads. Every networking event won't be in your best interest. Use your time attending quality events that will benefit you and your business.

Simply going to networking events to gather business cards isn't productive. This is what I like to call 'Business Card Quota' – whoever gets the most wins. Well, that's not wise and what happens is that you sacrifice quality for quantity.

Here are some ways you can add quality to your networking event:

- Find out in advance who some of the business owners will be in attendance.

- Refuse to be like so many networkers and simply grabs cards without conversation.

THE ABC'S OF MAKING BUSINESS NETWORKING WORK FOR YOU
RAPPORT

How many times have you heard the saying 'you have to build rapport with potential clients because people buy from people they know, like, and trust?' I wholeheartedly agree that building rapport is essential at any networking event. As I mentioned in the previous sections, you have to be confident and show initiative if you want your business to grow.

Building rapport with potential clients is more than having one or two things in common. It's about building trust. It goes without saying that people can read right through a salesperson. The typical salesperson is one who meets you at an event and is ready for you to sign a contract. No rapport built. This kind of salesperson is driven by numbers.

Entrepreneurs who are serious about their business and expanding their network understand that servicing a client extends after the sale. Through building rapport, you remain active in that person's mind and if you're really good, this person will send you referral after referral to help your business grow.

Here are some ways to build **GREAT** rapport:

- Drop the salesperson mentality. If you act like a salesperson, it will show on your face and come through in your voice.
- Understand that your objective is to meet people and find commonality.
- Look for ways to help. Let's face it – people remember those who go out of their way to help them.
- Don't act so formal. You don't have to be so uptight.

THE ABC'S OF MAKING BUSINESS NETWORKING WORK FOR YOU

STRATEGY

Strategically work/partner with someone you've met at prior events. By creating an alliance with someone and attending the same networking event together, you not only increase the number of people you meet, but you also receive validation through introduction.

Here are some ways in which you can form a strategic alliance with a fellow networker:

- Ask them if they are willing to work with you to maximize time and effectiveness.

- Make sure the two of you know each other well. Each of you should be credible.

- Work the room from different sides. In other words, you don't have to stand next to each other.

- Keep each other informed about entrepreneurs in the room.

Anytime you attend a networking event, you ought to have a plan. Here's a secret for you – the more networking events you attend; the more people you'll meet which will lead to an effective strategy to seeing your business succeed.

THE ABC'S OF MAKING BUSINESS NETWORKING WORK FOR YOU
TIMING

Everyone's time is valuable and you have to make sure you value it. Just as everyone's time is valuable during any networking event, so is yours. Unless you prioritize as well as maximize your time, you'll find yourself wasting time and being unproductive.

Here's something to be cautious about - an individual who makes it their business to draw you into long drawn-out conversation. They will prohibit you from meeting new people. Just as you don't want too much of your time occupied, have the same consideration for others.

Because timing is so crucial to getting an individual's undivided attention, you need to read their body language. If a person seems to be engaged in business via their phone or iPad, it's probably not wise to approach them. However, if an individual is looking around the room, this is the perfect time to approach them and win them over with your winning personality.

Here are some tips you can use to make your timing impeccable:

- Observe when people first enter the room at a networking event. Are they looking around confused or do they have some anxiety about them? If you sense something, approach them with light conversation.

- Check out who they're conversing with. If they're in a group, they may be drowned out with a whole lot of talk that isn't productive and/or stimulating. This is the ideal time to approach them and have them talk about themselves, their likes, and of course, their business.

Timing is everything. Position yourself as someone who enjoys what you're doing. Be respectful of other's time.

THE ABC'S OF MAKING BUSINESS NETWORKING WORK FOR YOU
UNDERSTAND

Without understanding why you do what you do, you'll come across as being confused. Let me ask you this. How many times have you asked someone about their business and they couldn't articulate it properly? Was it a turn off? Did you leave that conversation feeling more confused than ever and definitely telling yourself, I'm not going to do business with that person?

Every encounter with someone at a networking event requires you to listen to what the other person is saying. That way you'll know how to communicate what you can do to help that individual and his/her company. There's really no better or clearer way to say it - you need to understand your business, it's vision, and how it can help fulfill a need. No understanding means no success.

Networking with other professionals doesn't have to be difficult as long as you have an understanding of your business.

Here's what you need to do to have a better understanding of your business so that you won't squander opportunities:

- Constantly go over your vision statement along with why you're doing your specific business.

- Know what separates you and makes you unique from your competitors and be able to articulate it.

- Practice communicating your business with your family and friends. Don't give a sales pitch. If your family and friends can't understand what you do and how beneficial it is to them, how will a business owner grasp your business?

- Listen carefully and intently to the person talking to you. Don't be afraid to ask questions. As a matter of fact, when

THE ABC'S OF MAKING BUSINESS NETWORKING WORK FOR YOU

you ask questions, you get a clearer understanding of the other person's business.

Remember, if you don't understand why you're the best person to help fulfill a need, don't expect to get calls and don't expect to be in business long.

THE ABC'S OF MAKING BUSINESS NETWORKING WORK FOR YOU
VISIBLE

If people don't see you, they won't get a chance to know you. Attending networking events isn't about taking up space. I'm not saying to wear anything that will draw unwarranted attention to yourself. Nor am I saying to splash on the 'smell-good' too strong.

When you make yourself visible to people, they'll become more eager to want to know things about you. People have what is called discernment in that they can look at you and determine whether you want to be bothered or not. You don't ever want to appear as though you're disinterested. When you make yourself visible, you stand out from the crowd.

Here are some ways to make yourself more visible to the right people:

- Dress appropriately. People still judge others by how they're dressed. I know it sucks because people shouldn't judge, but in reality people still judge and will continue to judge.

- Be conscious of the vibe you give off. If you ever feel as though you're not giving off good energy, go into the restroom, take some deep breaths, talk to yourself to remind yourself that networking can be fun, and go back out and have a do over.

- Get out of dark areas. Stay in bright areas.

- Avoid being standoffish.

THE ABC'S OF MAKING BUSINESS NETWORKING WORK FOR YOU
WORK THE ROOM

I want you to get this in your spirit – you are at a networking event to meet people. The best way to meet people is to work the room. Clearly stated – make every effort you can to meet as many people as possible. Obviously this would be difficult at a large networking event, but an event with 20-40 people is sufficient for you to work.

While living in Maryland, I used to travel 5 ½ hours to attend a networking event in Pittsburgh, Pa. Even though I had a table set up to sell books, I understood that I could not sit at my table and simply wait for people to approach me. I would make it my mission to work the room, introduce myself, and point to my booth. The end result – SALES.

Working the room keeps you from being bored and stagnant. In addition to that, working the room keeps you on the move which will cause you to meet the right people who can help you directly and/or indirectly.

Here are some ways to work the room:

- Realize your time at a networking event isn't to be idle, but to meet people. You have to understand that it's your job to initiate the conversation and not sit back and wait for it to come to you.

- Understand your overall goal is to connect with people. Let's face it – you cannot connect with people if you're shy.

- Get into your spirit – you're the person people need to know. This isn't cockiness but confidence. When you know you're 'DA BOMB' you want others to know it also.

Be confident you are the person people need to know.

THE ABC'S OF MAKING BUSINESS NETWORKING WORK FOR YOU
XENOPHOBIA (AVOID)

The word Xenophobia is defined as "an intense or irrational dislike or fear of people from other countries." Sadly, other cultures are judged based on irrational myths. Judging will lead to ineffective networking. I don't care what anyone says, if you have a dislike of other people from different cultures, you're limiting your business growth. Entrepreneurs who are serious about growth understand that doing business globally is the way to go.

Because there are people from different ethnic groups and backgrounds who attend networking events, it's in your best interest to dispel any preconceived notions. The quicker you do it, the quicker you'll see doors of opportunity presented to you. You cannot let the media cause you to be biased. Nor should you listen to people who are judgmental and critical.

Here are some ways in which you can avoid xenophobia:

- Look in the mirror and address any biases and/or prejudices you may have.

- Avoid associating with people who negatively stereotype people and cultures. Their negativity will poison you.

- If you meet someone from another culture, ask them questions about their culture while talking about their business. This shows you're interested in learning about them and their country. Here's a hint: when you show interest, you are remembered and will stand out from the rest of the networkers.

Being successful in business means you're able to work with people from all walks of life without having misgivings based on culture, race, and ethnicity.

THE ABC'S OF MAKING BUSINESS NETWORKING WORK FOR YOU
YOU

This sounds really simply but it causes many people the most trouble. In order to become successful at any networking event, YOU Have to be there. No excuses. No procrastination. No hesitation. YOU have to be there in mind, body, and spirit. Let me ask you this. Have you ever met someone at a networking event and you could tell they weren't really there? Their body was present, but the rest of them wasn't.

There's so much potential in YOU. The mere fact that YOU decided to step out on faith and start your own business means YOU think enough of YOU to be a difference maker. Continue to believe in yourself.

With every networking event you have scheduled to attend, remember your dream. It's YOUR's. Use networking events to help YOU move closer to accomplishing it.

Here are some ways in which YOU can keep YOUR dreams alive:

- When talking with people, let them know why YOU do what you do. Make sure it's not about money because money doesn't translate to conviction.

- Evaluate and re-evaluate why YOU love doing what you do.

- Ask your business colleagues how they would describe you. When you hear from others how they see YOU as an entrepreneur, you'll get a glimpse of how people see YOU at networking events.

THE ABC'S OF MAKING BUSINESS NETWORKING WORK FOR YOU
ZEALOUS

To be zealous means you're eager to meet people. Now I understand that many people don't really look forward to attending networking events, especially more than 3 per week. But, I promise you, if you become zealous about all of the hidden possibilities and opportunities, you'll jump for joy every time you have the chance to network.

People are drawn to you if you're happy and eager to make things happen. When you exude happiness and confidence, people are drawn to you.

What you tell yourself inwardly has outward consequences. Your mind and spirit work together to produce either positive or negative reinforcement. That's why you must always water your mind and spirit with words of affirmation. Do this every day and you'll begin noticing a huge difference in how you interact with people, especially at networking events.

Here are some ways in which you can become zealous:

- Understand that a positive attitude attracts the right people to you.

- Determine that life is better when you choose to be happy compared to choosing to be angry and bitter.

- Know that happiness is contagious.

- Believe that you have every right to be successful and wealthy in your business.

- Remember why you decided to go into business.

www.ingramcontent.com/pod-product-compliance
Lightning Source LLC
Chambersburg PA
CBHW070421190526
45169CB00003B/1351